INDIAN RECIPES

✳

BALTI

The Publisher would like to thank
Hotel Holiday Inn Crown Plaza, New Delhi and
Maurya Sheraton Hotel and Towers, New Delhi
for the preparation of the dishes, and for giving
permission to photograph them.

© Lustre Press Pvt. Ltd. 1995
All rights reserved. No part of this publication may be reproduced
or transmitted in any form or by any means without
prior permission from the publishers

ISBN: 81-7437-038-2

Reprinted in 1998

First published by
Lustre Press Pvt. Ltd.,
M-75, GK II Market, New Delhi-110 048, INDIA
Phones: (011) 644 2271/6462782/646 0886 Fax: (011) 646 7185

Project Coordinator: Padmini Mehta
Photographs: Neeraj Paul & Dheeraj Paul
Design: Sarita Verma Mathur
Typesetting: Monika Gupta

Printed and bound by
Star Standard Industries Pte. Ltd., Singapore

INDIAN RECIPES
*
BALTI

Lustre Press
Delhi ◇ Banaras ◇ Agra ◇ Jaipur ◇ The Netherlands

INTRODUCTION

Balti cuisine—a new way of cooking hot, spicy curries—is being popularized by Indian chefs in the West. Several speciality Balti restaurants have opened in recent years to cater to the connoisseurs of Indian food.

A simple stir-fry method of cooking curries —lamb, fish, chicken and vegetarian —Balti uses a *karahi* (wok) to make a speedy, sumptuous Indian meal.

A *karahi* is a simple, round-bottomed pan with two ring handles. It is an Asian cook's favourite utensil and is commonly found in homes, shops and restaurants. Coming in various sizes, very large ones are used to cook for banquets while the sizzling hot food can be served at the table in the small ones. You will probably find that your own kitchen is well equipped with everything elseyou need to produce the dishes in this book. All the recipes can be cooked the traditional way in a *karahi* or a Balti pan, or just as effectively in a wok or deep frying pan.

Balti recipes included here range from Indian favourites adapted to this technique, to cuisine which has originated in northern Pakistan but has been influenced deeply by the cuisine of neighbouring India. The melange of Indian and Pakistani cuisines is truly inspiring. The results are fascinating according to the food enthusiasts.

BALTI
— ✳ —

Chicken

Kadhai Chicken	6
Chicken Khurchan	8
Dum ka Murgh	10
Masaledar Reshmi Tikka	11
Chicken Kastoori	12
Chicken Badam Pasanda	14
Sweet Sour Chicken	16
Dry Chilly Chicken	17
Chicken Navrattan Korma	18
Pepper Chicken	20
Murgh Begam-Bahar	22
Minced Chicken with Peas	23
Mughlai Murgh Shikanj	24

Fish

Sauce ni Machchi	26
Prawn Balchao	28
Garlic flavoured Prawns	30
Balti Pomfret	31
Fish in Tomato Sauce	32
Lobster Curry	34
Prawn Biryani	35

Lamb

Rara Meat	36
Lamb Mughlai	38
White Mince	40
Brain Curry	42
Lamb Chilli Fry	43
Cardamom flavoured Lamb	44
Kid nu Gosht	46

Vegetarian

Paneer Tawa Masala	48
Subz Jalfrezi	50
Gobhi Taka Tin	52
Kadhai Peas	54
Paneer Birbali	56
Smoked Aubergine	57
Banana Kofta	58
Vegetable Korma	60

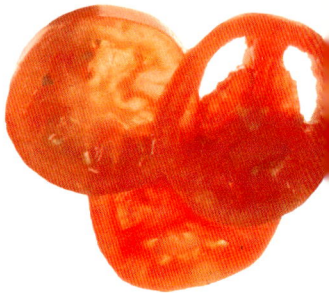

KADHAI CHICKEN

SERVES: 4

A tomato based chicken delicacy cooked in the Indian wok and flavoured strongly with fenugreek and coriander.

— Ingredients —

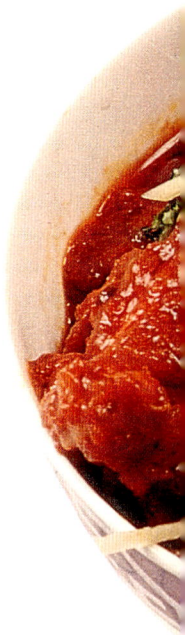

Chicken — *1 kg/2 birds, cut into 8 pieces each*
Coriander leaves *— 30 gms/ 2 tbs*
Coriander seeds, pounded *— 5 gms/1 tsp*
Garam masala *— 10 gms/2 tsp*
Garlic paste — *20 gms/4 tsp*
Ginger, chopped *— 45 gms/3 tbs*
Kasoori methi — *5 gms/1 tsp*
Green chillies, slit — *4*

Oil *— 80 ml/¹/₃ cup*
Red chillies, whole, pounded *— 8*
Salt to taste
Tomatoes, chopped *— 1 kg*

— Steps —

1. Heat oil in a kadhai. Sauté garlic paste till brown.

2. Add the pounded red chillies and the

6

freshly pounded coriander seeds and stir for a few seconds.

3. Add the tomatoes and bring to a boil.

4. Add half the coriander leaves and all the ginger, slit green chillies and salt. Simmer for 5 minutes.

5. Add the chicken and simmer, stirring occasionally till the gravy thickens and the chicken is tender.

6. Once the fat surfaces, stir in the garam masala and the kasoori methi. Cook for 2 minutes.

TIPS

Time: Preparation: 40 minutes
Cooking: 30 minutes

To serve: Garnish with coriander and serve with naan or roti.

CHICKEN KHURCHAN

SERVES: 4

*Shredded pre-cooked tandoori chicken stir-fried
and flavoured with real Indian spices.*

— Ingredients —

Tandoori chicken — *1*
Chaat masala — *5 gms/1 tsp*

Coriander leaves, chopped
— *5 gms/1 tsp*

Cooking oil — *5 ml/1 tsp*
Garam masala — *a pinch*
Ginger-garlic paste
— *5 gms/1 tsp*
Ginger juliennes
— *5 gms/1 tsp*
Green chilli, slit — *1*
Lemon juice — *15 ml/1 tbs*
Onion rings — *60 gms/¼ cup*
Red chilli powder — *a pinch*
Salt to taste
Tomatoes, chopped
— *25 gms/5 tsp*

— *Steps* —

1. Shred the tandoori chicken.
2. In a frying pan heat the oil and sauté onion rings.
3. Add ginger-garlic paste and slit green chilli.
4. Add the shredded chicken, salt, chaat masala, red chilli powder, garam masala and chopped coriander.
5. Stir-fry on medium flame.
6. Add lemon juice and chopped tomatoes. Fry for a few more minutes.

TIPS

Time:
Preparation: 20 minutes plus time to roast the chicken, if tandoori chicken is not available
Cooking: 10 minutes

To serve: Garnish with ginger juliennes and serve hot with any Indian bread and fresh salad.

DUM KA MURGH

SERVES: 4

Chicken cooked gently in its own juices!

— Ingredients —

Chicken (small, boneless cubes) — *1 kg*
Almond paste — *100 gms/½ cup*
Bay leaf (*tej patta*) — *1*
Butter, unsalted — *25 gms/5 tsp*
Cinnamon sticks — *5*
Cloves — *6*
Cream — *120 ml/⅔ cup*
Garlic paste — *25 gms/5 tsp*
Ginger paste — *25 gms/5 tsp*
Green cardamoms — *10*
Oil — *25 ml/1⅔ tbs*

Green chillies, slit into half — *6*
Mace powder (*javitri*) — *3 gms/⅔ tsp*
Mint leaves, fresh — *5 gms/1 tsp*
Onions, grated — *180 gms/¾ cup*
Red chilli powder — *10 gms/2 tsp*
Salt to taste
Turmeric powder (*haldi*) — *5 gms/1 tsp*
Vetivier (*kewda*) — *3 drops*

— Steps —

1. Heat the oil and butter in a pan. Add bay leaf, cinnamon, cloves and cardamoms and sauté over medium heat until they begin to crackle.

2. Add the onions and sauté for few minutes.

3. Add the ginger and garlic pastes, turmeric, red chilli powder, salt and almond paste and cook over medium heat for 5-10 minutes until the oil separates from the mixture.

4. Add the chicken, stir and cook over medium heat for 10-15 minutes.

5. Add the cream, green chillies, mace powder and vetivier.

6. Sprinkle with fresh mint leaves, cover and seal lid with a dough. Let the chicken simmer over very low heat for 5-6 minutes.

[It could also be kept in a preheated slow oven to 120 ºC (240 ºF) for 10 minutes. This is *dum* cooking.]

MASALEDAR RESHMI TIKKA

SERVES: 4

Sliced chicken in tomato gravy.

— Ingredients —

Chicken breast — *800 gms*
Crushed garlic
— *40 gms/2 tbs*
Green chillies, deseeded
— *4*
Oil — *40 ml/3 tbs*
Red chilli powder
— *3 gms/1 tbs*
Salt to taste

Sliced green pepper
— *60 gms/1*
Sliced onions — *150 gms/2-3*
Sliced tomatoes
— *100 gms/1-2*
Tomato paste
— *30 gms/2 tbs*
Turmeric powder
— *1 gm/1 tsp*

— Steps —

1. Cut boneless chicken breast into strips.
2. Heat oil in a large kadhai/*wok,* lower the heat and add crushed garlic and sliced onions. Stir fry for 1½ minute.
3. Add chicken strips and fry for 1 minute.
4. Mix in the red chilli powder, turmeric powder and tomato paste.
5. Add sliced green pepper, sliced tomatoes and slit and deseeded green chillies. Add salt and stir fry till chicken is cooked and sauce is coating.

CHICKEN KASTOORI

SERVES: 4

Tastes best with fresh fenugreek.

— Ingredients —

Chicken, boneless — *1 kg*
Bay leaves (*tej patta*) — *2*
Black cardamoms — *2*
Black cumin (*shah jeera*)
— *3 gms/²/₃ tsp*
Cinnamon sticks — *2*
Cloves — *8*
Coriander, chopped
— *15 gms/3 tsp*
Coriander powder
— *8 gms/1²/₃ tsp*
Fenugreek leaves, powdered
(*methi*)or — *15 gms/3 tsp*
Fresh fenugreek
— *200 gms/1 cup*
Garam masala
— *10 gms/2 tsp*
Garlic, chopped
— *30 gms/6 tsp*
Ginger, chopped —
50 gms/3¹/₃ tbs
Ginger juliennes —
10 gms/2 tsp

Green cardamoms — *10*
Green chillies, slit, deseeded
and chopped — *15 gms/3 tsp*
Mace powder (*javitri*)
— *5 gms/1 tsp*
Onions, chopped
— *30 gms/6 tsp*
Red chilli powder
— *8 gms/1²/₃ tsp*
Refined oil — *150 ml/³/₄ cup*
Tomatoes, chopped
— *180 gms/³/₄ cup*
Salt to taste

Turmeric powder (*haldi*)   Water — *240 ml/1¼ cups*
      — *5 gms/1 tsp*   Yoghurt — *225 gms/1¼ cups*

— *Steps* —

1. Cut the chicken into 15 pieces.

2. Whisk the yoghurt in a large bowl, add salt and marinade the chicken in this mixture for 30 minutes.

3. Heat the oil in a heavy bottomed pan. Add the whole spices (cardamoms, cloves, cinnamon sticks and bay leaves) and sauté over medium heat for a few minutes.

4. Add the black cumin, onions and sauté until golden brown.

5. Add garlic, ginger, green chillies, stir for 2 minutes. Add the turmeric, coriander and red chilli powder.

6. Add 60 ml (4 tbs) of water and stir for 30 seconds.

7. Add the tomatoes and cook over medium heat until the oil separates from the mixture.

8. Add the marinated chicken along with the marinade and 180 ml (¾ cup) of water, bring to a boil, cover and simmer until chicken is almost cooked and the oil separates from the sauce once again.

9. Adjust the seasoning.

10. Sprinkle fenugreek powder, mace powder, garam masala, ginger juliennes and green coriander. (If fresh fenugreek is used, chop and cook it with the chicken.) Cover and cook for 5 minutes more.

TIPS

Time: Preparation: 45 minutes
Cooking: 30 minutes

To serve: Serve hot, garnished with green coriander leaves and accompanied by rice or rotis.

CHICKEN BADAM PASANDA

SERVES: 4

A chicken steak with almonds.

— Ingredients —

Chicken breasts, skinned
— *8 pieces*
Almonds, sliced
— *25 gms/5 tsp*
Black pepper powder
— *2 gms/¹/₂ tsp*
Chicken stock — *1 ltr/5 cups*
Cloves — *10*
Flour — *10 gms/2 tsp*

Garlic paste
— *50 gms/3¹/₃ tbs*
Ghee (clarified butter)
— *100 gms/¹/₂ cup*
Ginger paste
— *50 gms/3¹/₃ tbs*
Green cardamoms — *10*
Green coriander
— *20 gms/4 tsp*

Mace powder (*javitri*)
— *2 gms/¹/₂ tsp*
Milk — *15 ml/1 tbs*
Onions, chopped
— *100 gms/¹/₂ cup*
Red chilli powder
— *5 gms/1 tsp*
Saffron (dissolved in 15 ml of
milk) — *1 gm*
Salt to taste
Tomatoes
— *250 gms/1 cup+3¹/₃ tbs*
Yoghurt (drained)
— *250 gms/1 cup+3¹/₃ tbs*

— *Steps* —

1. Brown the almonds in ghee.
2. Clean and flatten the chicken
breasts till about 3 cm thick.
3. Rub the ginger paste over the
chicken breasts.
4. Whisk the yoghurt in a large bowl and
add the garlic and salt, and rub this mixture
into the chicken. Keep aside for 1 hour.
5. Preheat the kadhai/*wok*. Pour half the ghee on it.
Place the chicken breasts on it, cook, turning over once
until half done. Remove from the *wok* and keep aside.
6. Add the remaining ghee to the *wok* and sauté green
cardamoms and cloves till they crackle. Then add
onions and cook till brown. Add tomatoes, red chilli
powder, flour, black pepper and chicken stock. Cook
until the gravy becomes rich and thick.
7. Place the chicken in the gravy and cook, turning it
over gently for another 10 minutes.
8. Add the mace powder and the saffron dissolved in a
little warm milk.

TIPS

Time: Preparation: 1¼ hours
Cooking: 20 minutes

To serve: Serve garnished with the fried
almonds and green coriander.

15

SWEET SOUR CHICKEN

SERVES: 4

Chicken chunks cooked in mango chutney.

— *Ingredients* —

Boneless chicken — *800 gms*
Butter — *3 tbs/40 gms*
Chilli powder — *1 tbs/3 gms*
Coriander powder
— *1 tbs/5 gms*
Cream — *4 tbs/60 ml*
Cumin powder — *1 tbs/4 gms*
Garlic (crushed)
— *1 tbs/15 gms*

Green chillies — *5 nos*
Ginger — *2 tbs/20 gms*
Salt to taste
Sweet mango chutney
— *2 tbs/30 gms*
Tomato puree
— *1 cup/60 gms*
Yoghurt — *½ cup/50 gms*

— *Steps* —

1. Cut boneless chicken into cubes (1 inch).
2. Make a paste with tomato puree, chilli powder, coriander and cumin powder, mango chutney, yoghurt garlic and salt in a blender.
3. Cut ginger into juliennes and deseed and slit green chillies.
4. Heat butter in a thick bottom wok. Pour the puree, bring to boil and simmer for 2 minutes.
5. Add chicken pieces and stir fry till chicken is cooked.
6. Finish by adding green chillies, ginger and cream.

TIPS

Time: Preparation: 15 minutes
Cooking: 15 minutes

To serve: Serve with pulao or naan.

DRY CHILLY CHICKEN

SERVE: 4

Spicy stir fried chicken.

— Ingredients —

Chicken boneless (cut into cubes) — *800 gms*
Chilli powder — *5 gms/1 tbs*
Coriander powder — *4 gms/1 tbs*
Coriander, fresh — *15 gms/2 tbs*
Fresh mint — *15 gms/2 tbs*
Garlic crushed — *40 gms/3 tbs*
Ginger paste — *40 gms/2½ tbs*
Green chillies — *8*
Lemon juice — *15 ml/1 tbs*
Oil — *45 ml/3 tbs*
Onion sliced — *100 gms/½ cup*
Salt to taste
Tomatoes, diced — *150 gms/2*

— Steps —

1. Cut chicken into strips.
2. Heat oil in a thick bottom wok. Add slit green chillies and fry until chillies change colour.
3. Add the onions, garlic-ginger paste, chilli powder, coriander powder and stir fry for a few seconds
4. Add chicken and stir fry for 7 minutes till chicken is cooked.
5. Sprinkle lemon juice, chopped coriander, mint and diced tomatoes.
6. Stir fry for 2 minutes on high flame.

TIPS

Time: Preparation: 25 minutes
Cooking: 15 minutes

To serve: Remove from fire and serve with naan or rotis.

Chicken Navrattan Korma

SERVES: 4

A rich curry garnished with dried fruits.

— Ingredients —

Chicken boneless/bone, 8 pieces — *1 kg*
Almond paste — *100 gms/¹/₂ cup*
Bay leaf (*tej patta*) — *1*
Butter, unsalted — *25 gms/5 tsp*
Cinnamon sticks — *5*
Cloves — *6*
Cream — *120 ml/²/₃ cup*
Garlic paste — *30 gms/6 tsp*
Ginger paste — *30 gms/6 tsp*
Green cardamoms — *10*
Green chillies, slit — *6*
Mace powder (*javitri*) — *3 gms/²/₃ tsp*
Onions, grated — *180 gms/³/₄ cup*
Red chilli powder — *10 gms/2 tsp*
Refined oil — *25 ml/1²/₃ tbs*
Salt to taste
Turmeric powder (*haldi*) — *5 gms/1 tsp*
Vetivier (*kewda*) — *3 drops*
Yoghurt, whisked — *20 gms/4 tsp*

18

For garnishing:
Almonds — *20 gms/4 tsp*
Black cumin seed (*shah jeera*), roasted and powdered — *3 gms/²/₃tsp*
Cashewnuts — *20 gms/4 tsp*
Fresh ginger juliennes — *1 gm/¹/₄ tsp*

Fresh mint leaves — *3 gms/²/₃ tsp*
Hazelnuts — *10 gms/2 tsp*
Pistachios — *15 gms/3 tsp*
Raisins — *10 gms/2 tsp*
Saffron strands, dissolved in 15 ml of warm milk — *3 gms/²/₃ tsp*

— Steps —

1. Fry the pistachios, cashewnuts, hazelnuts and almonds in a little butter for the garnish and keep aside.

2. Heat the oil and butter in the same pan. Add the bay leaf, cinnamon sticks, cloves and cardamoms, and sauté over medium heat until the spices begins to crackle.

3. Add the onions, and sauté for a few minutes. Add the ginger and garlic pastes, turmeric and red chilli powder, almond paste, salt and whisked yoghurt, and cook over medium heat for 5-10 minutes until the oil separates from the mixture.

4. Add the chicken, stir and cook over medium heat for 20-25 minutes till the chicken is cooked. Add cream, green chillies, mace powder and few drops of vetivier.

TIPS

Time: Preparation: 15 minutes
Cooking: 40 minutes

To serve: Garnish with sautéed nuts, raisins, ginger juliennes and saffron. Sprinkle with cumin powder, mint leaves. Serve hot with rice/rotis.

PEPPER CHICKEN

SERVES: 4

A South Indian chicken delicacy with pepper corns giving it a special flavour.

— Ingredients —

Chicken — *1.2 kg*
Black peppercorns — *20 gms/4 tsp*
Coriander leaves, chopped — *25 gms/5 tsp*
Garam masala — *5 gms/1 tsp*
Garlic paste — *45 gms/3 tbs*
Ginger paste — *45 gms/3 tbs*

Groundnut oil — *60 ml/4 tbs*
Lemon juice — *30 ml/2 tbs*
Onions, chopped — *180 gms/¾ cup*
Salt to taste
Tomatoes, chopped — *160 gms/²/₃ cup*
Yoghurt — *120 gms/½ cup*

— Steps —

1. Clean and cut the chicken into 8 pieces each.
2. Pound the peppercorns with a pestle.
3. Whisk the yoghurt and add the peppercorns, half the ginger and garlic pastes, lemon juice and salt. Mix well.
4. Marinade the chicken pieces in it for at least 30 minutes.
5. Meanwhile, heat oil in a handi. Add onions and sauté over medium heat until light brown.

6. Add the remaining ginger and garlic pastes and sauté until onions are golden brown.
7. Add the tomatoes and stir-cook till the fat appears on the sides of the pan.
8. Add the chicken along with the marinade and stir for 4-5 minutes. Add 240 ml/1 cup water and bring to boil.
9. Cover and let simmer, stirring occasionally until the chicken is tender.
10. Adjust the seasoning. Sprinkle garam masala and stir.

TIPS

Time: Preparation: 1 hour
Cooking: 30 minutes

To serve: Garnish with coriander leaves and serve with boiled rice or roti.

Murgh Begam-Bahar

SERVES: 4

Chicken curry garnished with lamb.

— Ingredients —

Chicken — *1 kg*	Lamb brain (par boiled)
Bay leaves (*tej patta*) — *2*	— *100 gms/½ cup*
Butter — *20 gms/4 tsp*	Oil — *80 ml/5⅓ tbs*
Cashewnut paste	Onions, chopped
— *100 gms/½ cup*	— *200 gms/1 cup*
Cinnamon sticks (1 cm) — *3*	Red chilli powder
Cloves — *8*	— *8 gms/1⅔ tsp*
Cream — *80 ml/5⅓ tbs*	Salt — *15 gms/3 tsp*
Fenugreek (*methi*) powder	Turmeric powder (*haldi*)
— *2 gms/½ tsp*	— *6 gms/1⅓ tsp*
Garam masala	Yoghurt, whisked
— *15 gms/3 tsp*	— *150 gms/¾ cup*
Garlic paste — *25 gms/5 tsp*	For parboiling the brain:
Ginger paste — *25 gms/5 tsp*	Salt — *10 gms/2 tsp*
Green cardamoms — *8*	Turmeric (*haldi*)
Green coriander, chopped	— *5 gms/1 tsp*
— *15 gms/3 tsp*	Water — *½ litre*
Hot water — *30 ml/2 tbs*	

— Steps —

1. Clean and skin the chicken and cut into 8 pieces.
2. Heat the oil in a heavy bottomed pan over low heat. Add bay leaves, cinnamon sticks, green cardamoms and cloves. Sauté over medium heat till they crackle.
3. Add the chopped onions, turmeric powder and red chilli powder and sauté for another 30 seconds.
4. Add the ginger and garlic pastes, cashewnut paste, and sauté for another 30 seconds.
5. Add the chicken pieces, stir and cook for 10-15 minutes on medium heat.
6. Add the salt and yoghurt. Add hot water. Cover and simmer for 10 minutes on low heat. Add the cream, garam masala and fenugreek powder.
7. For parboiling the brain, bring the water to boil along with the salt and turmeric. Add the lamb brain and lower heat. Once the brain rises to the top, remove it

from the pan and keep aside.

8. In another pan, heat the butter. Sauté the lamb brain for 2-3 minutes. Break it up with the help of a spoon.

TIPS

Time: Preparation: 15 minutes
Cooking: 30 minutes

To serve: Transfer the chicken to a serving dish, and garnish with the fried brain and chopped green coriander.

MINCED CHICKEN WITH PEAS

SERVE : 4

An easy to cook chicken

— Ingredients —

Chicken, minced — *2½ cups/600 gms*
Boiled egg — *2*
Butter — *3 tbs/45 gms*
Cumin seeds — *1 tsp/4 gms*
Dry red chillies crushed — *10 gms*
Garlic (peeled and crushed) — *2 tbs/40 gms*

Ginger paste — *2 tbs/30 gms*
Green coriander — *2 tbs/15 gms*
Green peas — *1½ cups/250 gms*
Onions chopped — *1 cup/40 gms*
Tomato paste — *3 tbs/45g*
Salt to taste

— Steps —

1. Heat butter in a thick bottom wok. Splutter cumin seeds, add onions and stir fry till onions are brown.
2. Add chicken mince, crushed garlic, ginger paste, crushed dry red chillies salt and tomato paste
3. Stir fry till butter appears on top.
4. Add green peas and stir fry till dry and cook till golden brown in colour.

TIPS

Time: Preparation: 25 minutes
Cooking: 15 minutes

To serve: Remove and serve garnished with chopped green coriander and diced boiled eggs.

Mughlai Murgh Shikanj

SERVES: 4

Egg and cheese-coated chicken legs.

— Ingredients —

Chicken drumsticks, skinned and deboned — *5*

Black pepper, crushed — *5 gms/1 tsp*

Butter — *40 gms/2²/₃ tbs*

Cornflour — *20 gms/4 tsp*

Cottage cheese (*paneer*), grated — *50 gms/3¹/₃ tbs*

Cream — *40 ml/2²/₃ tbs*

Eggs — *2*

Garam masala — *5 gms/1 tsp*

Ghee (clarified butter) — *100 gms/¹/₂ cup*

Green chilli paste — *5 gms/1 tsp*

Lemon juice — *3 ml/²/₃ tsp*

Mace powder (*javitri*)	Salt to taste
— *3 gms/²/₃ tsp*	Yoghurt (drained)
Nutmeg powder (*jaiphal*)	— *80 gms/5¹/₃ tbs*
— *3 gms/²/₃ tsp*	

— *Steps* —

1. With a steak hammer flatten the deboned chicken drumsticks and arrange them on a platter.

2. Make a paste of the nutmeg, black pepper, garam masala and green chillies. Rub the paste on the chicken pieces. Keep aside for an hour.

3. In a bowl combine all the other ingredients to a fine creamy consistency.

4. Marinate the chicken in this mixture for ½ hour.

5. Heat the ghee in a pan over medium heat, and shallow fry the chicken pieces till crisp and golden.

TIPS

Time: Preparation: 1½ hours
Cooking: 15 minutes

To serve: Serve accompanied by lemon wedges, green salad and mint chutney.

Sauce ni Machchi

SERVES: 4

A tangy, easy to make, light fish dish.

— Ingredients —

Shrimp and pomfret darnes — 600 gms

Chilli powder — 2.5 gms/½ tsp

Coriander leaves, chopped — 30 gms/2 tsp

Cumin (*jeera*) seeds — 2.5 gms/½ tsp

Eggs, whipped — 2

Garlic, chopped — 10 gms/2 tsp

Gram flour (*besan*) — 25 gms/5 tsp

Green chillies, chopped — 4

Oil — 45 ml/3 tbs

Sugar — 25 gms/5 tsp

Tomatoes, chopped — 225 gms/1 cup

Vinegar — 120 ml/½ cup

For khichdi:

Basmati rice — 125 gms/½ cup

Cumin (*jeera*) seeds — 2.5 gms/½ tsp

Clarified butter (*ghee*) — 15 ml/1 tbs

Fenugreek (*methi*) seeds — 2.5 gms/½ tsp

Lentils — *60 gms/¼ cup*
Onions, sliced
— *60 gms/¼ cup*

Turmeric (*haldi*) powder
— *5 gms/1 tsp*

— *Steps* —

1. Apply salt to the fish and set aside for 10 minutes.
2. Heat the oil in a kadhai and fry garlic till pink.
3. Add cumin, coriander leaves, chillies and gram flour.
Sauté together till light brown.
4. Add the chopped tomatoes, 0.5 litre/2 cups water
and cook for 4 minutes. Season.
5. Add the fish and cook for 2-3 minutes. Remove from
fire.
6. Whisk the eggs with sugar and vinegar, then heat the
mixture in another pan. Add to the fish and gravy.
Return the kadhai to very low heat and cook for 6
minutes.
For the khichdi:
Wash rice and lentils in plenty of water, then soak for
15 minutes. Fry onions in the ghee till brown. Add
turmeric, cumin and fenugreek and sauté. Drain
rice and lentils and add to the pan. Fry for 3-4
minutes. Add 360 ml/1½ cups boiling water, cover
and cook till rice and lentils are well mashed, about
10-15 minutes.

TIPS

Time: Preparation: 30 minutes
Cooking: 30 minutes

To serve: Serve fish with khichdi, pickles and
poppadams.

27

Prawn Balchao

SERVES: 4

This is a favourite Goan dish which can be preserved for a couple of days. In fact, its tangy taste is at its best after a day or so. It can be stored as a pickle for longer, if preservatives are added.

— Ingredients —

Prawns, small size — *1 kg*
Black peppercorns — *2.5 gms/½ tsp*
Cardamoms — *12*
Cinnamon — *4 sticks, 1" each*
Cloves — *5 gms/15*
Cumin (*jeera*) seeds — *2.5 gms/½ tsp*
Curry leaves — *12*
Garlic paste — *30 gms/2 tbs*
Ginger paste — *15 gms/1 tbs*

Groundnut oil — *160 ml/⅔ cup*
Malt vinegar — *160 ml/⅔ cup*
Onions, chopped — *160 gms/⅔ cup*
Red chillies, whole — *15*
Sugar — *25 gms/5 tsp*
Tomatoes, chopped — *120 gms/½ cup*

— Steps —

1. Shell, devein, wash and pat dry prawns.

2. Blend the peppercorns, cardamoms, cinnamon, cloves, cumin and red chillies with the vinegar in a blender. Keep aside.

3. Heat oil in a kadhai and deep fry prawns to a golden brown. Remove.

4. Add the onions to the hot oil. Sauté till golden brown.

5. Add the ginger and garlic pastes and stir for a minute.

6. Add the tomatoes and the blended paste.

7. Stir for 2-3 minutes.

8. Add the fried prawns, curry leaves and sugar and cook till prawns are tender.

TIPS

Time:
Preparation: 30 minutes
Cooking: 30 minutes

To serve: Serve hot with steamed rice or any Indian bread.

GARLIC FLAVOURED PRAWNS

SERVES: 4.

Prawns uniquely flavoured with garlic.

— Ingredients —

Prawns (medium size) — *1 kg*
Garlic — *4 tbs/100 gms*
Green chillies — *5*
Lemon juice — *4 tbs/60 ml*

Mustard seeds — *1 tsp/10 gms*
Oil — *3 tbs/45 ml*
Onions — *2-3/250 gms*
Salt to taste
Yoghurt — *¾ cup/100 gms*

— Steps —

1. Peel, devein & clean prawns. Chop onions and crush garlic.

2. Heat oil in a deep round bottom frying pan. Add mustard seeds and fry till they crackles.

3. Throw in the garlic and onions & stir fry till onions are soft. Add slit & deseeded green chillies.

4. Add prawns and stir fry till prawns are half cooked (1½ minutes)

5. Lower the heat and add lemon juice and whisked yoghurt. Season to taste.

TIPS

Time: Preparation: 25 minutes
Cooking: 10 minutes

To serve: Serve with boiled rice.

BALTI POMFRET

SERVES: 4

Fish fillets coated with spicy mixture.

— Ingredients —

Pomfret fillet — *800 gms*
Coriander green
— *12 tbs/200 gms*
Coriander powder
— *1 tbs/3 gms*
Green chillies — *10*
Malt vinegar — *3 tbs/60 ml*

Mint — *3 tbs/50 gms*
Oil for frying
Red chilli powder
— *1 tbs/3 gms*
Salt to taste
Tamarind — *1 tbs/50 gms*

— Steps —

1. Rub pomfret fillets with salt and malt vinegar.
2. Soak tamarind in hot water and take out pulp.
3. Make a paste in a blender with red chilli powder, green chillies, coriander powder, mint, green coriander and tamarind pulp.
4. Marinate the pomfret fillet in the paste and keep aside for half an hour. Heat oil in a non stick pan and pan fry the fillets coated with the marinade till crisp.

TIPS

Time: Preparation: 30 minutes
Cooking: 10 minutes

To serve: Remove and serve with bread or rice.

FISH IN TOMATO SAUCE

SERVES: 4

A fish preparation which literally melts in the mouth.

— Ingredients —

Sole fish fillets — *600 gms*
Cashew nuts — *10 gms/2 tsp*
Red chilli powder
 — *10 gms/2 tsp*
Coconut, grated
 — *10 gms/2 tsp*
Coriander leaves, chopped
 — *10 gms/2 tsp*

Cream — *80 ml/¹/₃ cup*
Garam masala — *5 gms/1 tsp*
Garlic paste — *10 gms/2 tsp*
Garlic, peeled and chopped
 — *25 gms/5 tsp*
Ginger paste — *15 gms/1 tbs*
Lemon juice — *30 ml/2 tbs*
Oil — *120 ml/¹/₂ cup*

Salt to taste
Sunflower seeds
— *10 gms/2 tsp*
Tomatoes, chopped
— *300 gms/1¼ cups*

— *Steps* —

1. Marinade the
fish in a mixture of
the ginger and garlic
pastes, salt, lemon
juice and half the chilli
powder. Set aside for half an
hour.
2. Meanwhile, grind coconut, sunflower seeds and
cashew nuts in a mixer.
3. Heat oil in a handi. Add fish and sauté lightly. Set
aside.
4. In the remaining hot oil add the peeled garlic and
sauté till golden brown.
Add the tomatoes and stir-cook till the tomatoes are
mashed.
5. Stir in the salt, left over red chilli powder and cook
for 5 minutes.
6. Strain the gravy through a strainer and put on fire
again.
7. Add the coconut, sunflower seed and cashew nut
paste, stir for 2-3 minutes.
8. Add the garam masala and the fried fish. Reserve 2
tablespoons cream for garnish and add the rest to the
gravy. Let simmer for 2-3 minutes.

TIPS

Time: Preparation: 45 minutes
Cooking: 30 minutes

To serve: Garnish with fresh coriander leaves
and cream. Serve hot with boiled rice.

LOBSTER CURRY

SERVES: 4

A traditional south Indian curry

— Ingredients —

Lobster — *800 gms/1¾ lb*
Chopped coriander
— *3 gms/1 tbs*
Coconut paste
— *60 gms/3 tbs*
Cooking oil — *90 ml/6 tbs*
Curry leaves — *10*
Garlic paste
— *15 gms/2½ tsp*
Ginger paste
— *15 gms/2½ tsp*
Green chillies chopped — *4*

Lemon juice
— *15 ml/1 tbs*
Onion, chopped
— *90 gms/½ cup*
Red chilli powder
— *5 gms/1 tsp*
Salt to taste
Tomatoes, chopped
— *120 gms/¾ cup*
Turmeric (*haldi*)
— *5 gms/1 tsp*

— Steps —

1. Shell, devein, wash and cut lobsters into dices.
2. Heat oil in a pan and sauté onion till golden brown.
3. Add the ginger and garlic paste and sauté till brown.
4. Add green chillies, chilli powder, turmeric powder salt and tomatoes. Stir cook till the masala mix leaves the sides of the pan.
5. Add the diced lobsters. Sauté for 2-3 minutes.
6. Stir in the coconut paste. Add approximately 2 cups/ 500 ml water and bring to boil.
7. Reduce flame and simmer.
8. Add lemon juice, curry leaves and cook for 2-3 minutes.

TIPS

Time: Preparation: 30 minutes
Cooking: 30 minutes

To serve: Remove to a bowl and garnish with chopped coriander. Serve with steaming hot boiled rice.

PRAWN BIRYANI

SERVES: 4

A whole meal in itself, can be served with yoghurt as an accompaniment.

— Ingredients —

Rice — *2½ cups/500 gms*
Prawns — *10/400 gms*
Bay leaf — *2*
Butter — *4 tbs/60 gms*
Cardamoms — *4*
Capsicum (slices) — *1 cup/100 gms*
Cinnamon — *2*
Onions (chopped) — *1 cup/100 gms*
Peppercorns — *10*
Saffron (dissolved in 1 tbs milk) — *1 gm*
Tomato (slices) — *100 gms/2*

— Steps —

1. Wash rice and soak for 15 minutes.
2. Peel, devein and clean prawns.
3. Soak saffron in 30 ml hot water.
4. Heat butter in a thick bottom pan. Add cardamoms, peppercorns, bay leaf and cinnamon and stir.
5. Lower the heat and add onions, capsicum, tomatoes and prawns. Fry for 1 minute and add the rice.
6. Add 1 litre water and bring to a boil. Cover the pan and simmer till water is absorbed and holes are formed on the surface of the rice. Add saffron and bake in an oven for 7-8 minutes.

TIPS

Time: Preparation: ½ hour
Cooking: ½ hour

To serve: Mix gently and serve hot with raita, pappadam and pickles.

Rara Meat

SERVES: 4

Lamb stir-cooked in a spicy gravy.

— Ingredients —

Lamb cuts — *1 kg*
Bay leaves (*tej patta*) — *2*
Black cardamoms — *3*
Cardamoms — *8*
Coriander powder — *25 gms/5 tsp*
Cumin (*jeera*) powder — *10 gms/2 tsp*
Garlic, chopped — *20 gms/4 tsp*
Garlic paste — *45 gms/3 tbs*
Ginger, shredded — *20 gms/4 tsp*

Ginger paste — *45 gms/3 tbs*
Oil — *160 gms/²/₃ cup*
Onions, chopped — *240 gms/1 cup*
Red chilli powder — *5 gms/1 tsp*
Red chillies, whole — *4*
Salt to taste
Tomatoes, chopped — *160 gms/²/₃ cup*
Turmeric (*haldi*) powder — *2.5 gms/¹/₂ tsp*
Yoghurt — *160 gms/²/₃ cup*

— Steps —

1. Whisk together the yoghurt and salt and marinade the lamb in it for an hour.

2. Heat the oil in a pot and crackle bay leaves and both the cardamoms in it.

3. Add the onions and sauté till light brown.

4. Add ginger and garlic pastes and stir for 4 to 5 minutes.

5. Stir in coriander, turmeric and red chilli powders.

6. Add the lamb with the marinade, bring to boil then reduce flame. Let simmer, adding 3 teaspoons of water at intervals. Cook until tender.

7. Add the tomatoes, chopped garlic and ginger and stir.

8. Then add the cumin and whole red chillies. Cook on low flame till the lamb pieces are coated with the masala and are tender.

TIPS

Time: Preparation: 1½ hours
Cooking: 1½ hours

To serve: Serve with any Indian bread.

Lamb Mughlai

SERVES: 4

A delicately flavoured lamb curry.

— Ingredients —

Lamb (boneless cubes) — *1 kg*
Bay leaf (*tej patta*) — *1*
Black pepper — *2 gms/¹/₂ tsp*

Cashewnut paste — *300 gms/1¹/₂ cups*
Cinnamon sticks — *4*
Cloves — *8*

Egg, boiled — *1*

Garlic paste
— *50 gms/3¹/₃ tbs*

Ginger paste
— *50 gms/3¹/₃ tbs*

Green cardamoms — *6*

Green chilli paste
— *50 gms/3¹/₃ tbs*

Refined oil — *200 gms/1 cup*

Saffron — *2 gms*

Salt to taste

Yoghurt, whisked
— *100 gms/¹/₂ cup*

— *Steps* —

1. Heat the oil. Add the cinnamon, cardamoms, cloves and bay leaf and sauté over medium heat for 30 seconds.

2. Add the ginger, garlic and green chilli pastes. Cook thoroughly.

3. Add the yoghurt and lamb cubes and cook on a low fire for 45 minutes.

4. When meat is tender, add the cashewnut paste, salt, pepper and saffron. Stir briefly and remove from heat.

Note: Chicken Mughlai can also be made using the same ingredients and method, substituting chicken for the lamb.

TIPS

Time: Preparation: 15 minutes
Cooking: 1 hour

To serve: Serve garnished with a boiled egg.

WHITE MINCE

SERVES: 4

The uniqueness of this preparation lies in the fact that red meat turns into a white gravy dish.

— Ingredients —

Lamb mince — 750 gms
Almonds — 15 gms/1 tbs
Cardamom powder — 2.5 gms/½ tsp
Cashew nuts — 15 gms/1 tbs
Cooking oil — 60 ml/4 tbs
Garlic, chopped — 15 gms/1 tbs
Green chillies, whole — 4
Onions, chopped — 80 gms/⅓ cup
Poppy seeds (*khus khus*) — 15 gms/3 tsp
White pepper powder — 5 gms/1 tsp
Yoghurt — 240 gms/1 cup

— Steps —

1. Soak and peel almonds.
2. Soak cashew nuts and poppy seeds for an hour and blend all three with a little water to a fine paste.
3. Heat oil in a kadhai and sauté onions and garlic on low flame without letting them turn brown.
4. Add mince and sauté over gentle heat.
5. Whisk and add the yoghurt, cardamom powder, white pepper powder and whole green chillies.
6. Simmer gently till mince is cooked and gravy is reduced by half.

7. Pick out and discard the green chillies.
8. Add the nut paste and stir well. Simmer for 2-3 minutes.

Brain Curry

SERVES: 4

Lamb brains cooked to get a dark, thick, gravy.

— Ingredients —

Lamb brains — *6, each 100 gms*
Black pepper powder — *2.5 gms/½ tsp*
Chilli powder — *5 gms/1 tsp*
Cooking oil — *90 ml/6 tbs*
Coriander leaves, chopped — *5 gms/1 tbs*
Coriander powder — *10 gms/2 tsp*
Fenugreek (*kasoori methi*) leaves, dry, rubbed — *2.5 gms/½ tsp*
Salt to taste

Fenugreek (*methe*) seeds — *2.5 gms/½ tsp*
Garam masala — *2.5 gms/½ tsp*
Garlic paste — *10 gms/2 tsp*
Ginger juliennes — *5 gms/1 tsp*
Ginger paste — *10 gms/2 tsp*
Lemon juice — *60 ml/4 tbs*
Onion paste — *105 gms/7 tbs*
Turmeric (*haldi*) powder — *10 gms/2 tsp*
Yoghurt — *120 gms/½ cup*

— Steps —

1. Immerse the brains in water with half the turmeric, 3 tablespoons lemon juice and half of the ginger and garlic pastes and salt.

2. Bring to boil. Simmer for 10 minutes then remove brains carefully.

3. Whisk yoghurt with the remaining turmeric, ginger and garlic pastes, chilli powder and onion paste.

4. Heat oil in a kadhai and crackle the fenugreek seeds. Add coriander powder and the yoghurt mixture and stir-fry until oil surfaces.

5. Add the brains and half cup water. Cover and cook for 4-5 minutes.

6. Add garam masala, black pepper and fenugreek leaves. Cook on low heat for 2 minutes.

TIPS

Time: Preparation: 20 minutes
Cooking: 30 minutes

To serve: Garnish with chopped coriander, ginger juliennes and sprinkle with lemon juice.

LAMB CHILLI FRY

SERVES: 4

A quick stir fried lamb delicacy.

— Ingredients —

Lamb, cleaned, washed and sliced — *900 gms*
Cumin, roasted and powdered (*jeera*) — *5 gms/1 tsp*
Garlic paste — *50 gms/3¹/₃ tbs*
Ginger paste — *50 gms/3¹/₃ tbs*
Lemon juice — *30 ml/2 tbs*
Green and red chillies, slit in half — *50 gms each*

Green coriander, chopped — *10 gms/2 tsp*
Oil — *100 ml/½ cup*
Onion rings or spring onions — *200 gms/1 cup*
Red chilli powder — *10 gms/2 tsp*
Salt for seasoning
Turmeric powder (*haldi*) — *10 gms/2 tsp*
Water or stock — *100 ml/¹/₂ cup*

— Steps —

1. Mix together the ginger and garlic pastes, turmeric powder, red chilli powder, salt and 3 tbs of oil.
2. Marinate the lamb in this mixture for at least 4-5 hours or, preferably, overnight.
3. Heat the oil in a kadhai/wok to smoking point. Put the marinated lamb into the wok, stir fry on a high heat for 4-5 minutes.
4. Sprinkle half a cup of water or stock on the lamb, stirring once or twice. Add the red and green chillies and onions rings, stir and cook for 2-3 minutes.
5. Season to taste with salt and lemon juice. Sprinkle with roasted cumin powder.

TIPS

Time: Preparation: 5 hours
Cooking: 45 minutes

To serve: Serve garnished with green coriander, with raita and any Indian bread.

CARDAMOM FLAVOURED LAMB

SERVES: 4

Usually known as Gosht Kalia due to the silver leaf and saffron which sets off the creamy gravy beneath.

— Ingredients —

Lamb curry cuts — *900 gms*
Almond paste — *30 gms/2 tbs*
Cardamom powder
— *5 gms/1 tsp*
Fresh cream — *30 ml/2 tbs*
Garlic paste — *10 gms/2 tsp*
Ginger paste — *10 gms/2 tsp*
Green chillies, chopped — *2*
Onions, chopped
— *90 gms/6 tbs*
Saffron — *a pinch*
Salt to taste
Silver leaf
Sweet ittar — *a few drops*
White butter — *60 gms/¼ cup*
Yoghurt — *60 gms/¼ cup*

— Steps —

1. Put lamb cuts in a pan of water and bring to boil. Drain and wash pieces.
2. Put the blanched lamb pieces, together with chopped onions, ginger and garlic pastes, yoghurt, butter, chillies, salt and half the cardamom powder in a pan and simmer. Ensure that the meat does not sear unevenly. Cook till lamb is tender.
3. Add the almond paste and cook till the gravy thickens.
4. Finish off by adding the rest of the cardamom powder, sweet ittar and cream.

TIPS

Time: Preparation: 30 minutes
Cooking: 1½ hours

To serve: Remove to a serving dish,
place silver leaf on top and sprinkle with
saffron crushed in a teaspoonful of water.
Serve with any Indian bread.

KID NU GOSHT

SERVES: 4

A combination of lamb and potatoes cooked in a spicy gravy.

— Ingredients —

Lamb — *500 gms*
Bay leaf (*tej patta*) — *1*
Black peppercorns
— *2.5 gms/½ tsp*
Cashew nuts
— *80 gms/⅓ cup*
Cinnamon — *2" stick*
Cloves — *4*
Coconut milk
— *240 ml/1 cup*
Cooking oil — *80 ml/⅓ cup*
Cumin (*jeera*) seeds
— *2.5 gms/½ tsp*

Garlic paste
— *10 gms/2 tsp*
Ginger paste
— *10 gms/2 tsp*
Green chillies
— *4*
Onions, chopped
— *160 gms/⅔ cup*
Salt to taste
Poppy seeds
— *2.5 gms/½ tsp*
Potatoes, diced
— *180 gms/¾ cup*

— Steps —

1. Marinade the lamb in half the ginger and garlic pastes for 2 hours.

2. In a non-stick pan heat the oil and sauté the onions till reddish brown.

3. Add the remaining ginger and garlic pastes, cumin seeds, salt, poppy seeds, cashew nuts, green chillies and the whole spices (cinnamon, cloves and black peppercorns).

4. Sauté for 5 minutes on a moderate flame.

5. Add meat pieces and sauté for 8-10 minutes. Every few minutes sprinkle with a tablespoon of water to keep contents of the pan moist.

6. Add 0.5 litre/2 cups water and potatoes. Cover and stew till meat is tender.

46

7. Add the coconut milk, simmer for a minute then remove from fire.

Note: Lamb shanks are ideal for this dish. However, any stewing cuts or 2" pieces are suitable.

TIPS

Time: Preparation: 2¼ hours
Cooking: 1½ hours

To serve: Serve hot with steamed rice.

PANEER TAWA MASALA

SERVES: 4

This is a unique preparation of cottage cheese cooked on a griddle.

— Ingredients —

Cottage cheese (*paneer*), cubed — *450 gms*
Black cumin (*shah jeera*) seeds — *2.5 gms/¹⁄₂ tsp*
Carom (*ajwain*) seeds — *1 gm/a pinch*
Capsicum, diced — *120 gms/¹⁄₂ cup*
Coriander powder — *10 gms/2 tsp*
Coriander leaves, chopped — *15 gms/1 tbs*
Cumin (*jeera*) seeds — *5 gms/1 tsp*
Garam masala — *1 gm/a pinch*
Garlic paste — *25 gms/5 tsp*
Ginger paste — *25 gms/5 tsp*
Ginger juliennes — *5 gms/1 tsp*
Green chillies, chopped — *2*
Oil — *45 ml/3 tbs*
Oil to fry the cheese

Onions, chopped — *180 gms/³⁄₄ cup*
Red chilli powder — *5 gms/1 tsp*
Salt to taste
Tomatoes, chopped — *180 gms/³⁄₄ cup*
White pepper powder — *5 gms/1 tsp*

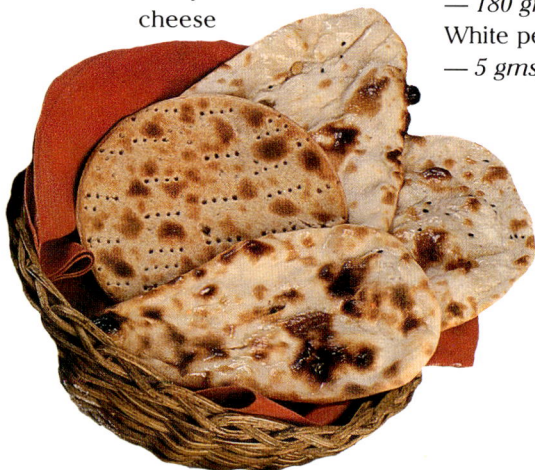

— Steps —

1. Heat oil in a kadhai and fry the cottage cheese to golden.

2. Heat the griddle. Add 3 tablespoons oil. When oil is hot add cumin and splutter.
3. Add the chopped onions and brown.
4. Add ginger and garlic pastes, green chillies, coriander powder, red chilli powder, white pepper powder, salt and carom seeds. Fry on medium heat.

5. Add chopped tomatoes. Fry till the oil surfaces.
6. Mix in the cottage cheese, capsicum, garam masala, black cumin and cook for 5 minutes.

TIPS

Time: Preparation: 10 minutes
Cooking: 15 minutes

To serve: Garnish with chopped coriander and ginger juliennes. Serve hot with any Indian bread.

SUBZ JALFREZI

SERVES: 4

A vegetarian delicacy. Hot peppercorn, lemon curry.

— Ingredients —

Button mushrooms — *150 gms/³⁄₄ cup*
Button onions — *150 gms/³⁄₄ cup*
Capsicum (*green pepper*) — *150 gms/³⁄₄ cup*
Carrots — *150 gms/³⁄₄ cup*
Cauliflower, cut into small flowerets — *150 gms/³⁄₄ cup*
Potatoes — *150 gms/³⁄₄ cup*
Cumin powder (*jeera*) — *3 gms/²⁄₃ tsp*
Garam masala — *15 gms/3 tsp*
Ginger juliennes — *20 gms/4 tsp*
Green cardamoms — *5*
Green chillies, slit — *15 gms/3 tsp*
Green coriander, chopped — *15 gms/3 tsp*
Oil — *80 ml/5¹⁄₃ tbs*
Onions, chopped — *100 gms/¹⁄₂ cup*
Red chilli powder — *10 gms/2 tsp*
Red chillies, whole — *5*
Salt to taste
Sugar — *5 gms/1 tsp*
Tomatoes, chopped — *150 gms/³⁄₄ cup*
Turmeric powder (*haldi*) — *8 gms/1²⁄₃ tsp*
Vinegar, white — *30 ml/2 tbs*
White pepper powder — *5 gms/1 tsp*

— Steps —

1. Heat the oil in a pan, add green cardamoms and whole red chillies and sauté over medium heat until they begin to crackle.
2. Add chopped onions and sauté until light brown.
3. Add the turmeric powder, red chilli powder, white pepper and cumin powder and sauté for 30 seconds.
4. Cut the capsicum into long strips and add them to

potatoes, carrots, button onions, cauliflower, tomatoes
and button mushrooms and sauté for another 30
seconds over high heat.

5. Add the sugar, vinegar and garam masala and sauté
for 30 seconds.

6. Cover and cook for 6 minutes.

TIPS

Time: Preparation: 10 minutes
Cooking: 15 minutes

To serve: Season with salt. Garnish with green
chillies, ginger julienne and green coriander.

GOBHI TAKA TIN

SERVES: 4

***Fried cauliflower, cooked with capsicum and
tomato in masala.***

— Ingredients —

Cauliflower — *500 gms*
Capsicum, cubed
— *100 gms/1 large*
Coriander leaves, chopped
— *5 gms/1 tbs*
Cumin (*jeera*) powder
— *10 gms/2 tsp*
Cumin (*jeera*) seeds
— *2.5 gms/¹/₂ tsp*
Garam masala
— *15 gms/1 tbs*
Garlic paste — *45 gms/3 tbs*
Green chillies, chopped
— *25 gms/8*
Ginger juliennes
— *10 gms/2 tsp*

Ginger
paste —
*45 gms/
3 tbs*
Kasoori
methi — *10 gms/2 tsp*
Oil — *160 ml/²/₃ cup*
Onions, chopped
— *180 gms/³/₄ cup*
Red chilli powder
— *20 gms/4 tsp*
Salt to taste
Tomatoes, cubed
— *240 gms/1 cup*
Yoghurt — *120 gms/¹/₂ cup*

— Steps —

1. Break the cauliflower into small florets.
2. Heat oil in a kadhai. Fry the cauliflower and keep
aside.
3. In the same oil add cumin seeds. When they begin to
crackle add chopped onions. Fry till golden brown.
4. Add the ginger and garlic pastes, green chillies, salt,
chilli powder, cumin

powder, garam masala, kasoori methi and yoghurt. Stir-fry.

5. Add capsicum and tomato cubes and fry again.

6. Add cauliflower and simmer for 5 minutes.

TIPS

Time: Preparation: 25 minutes
Cooking: 25 minutes

To serve: Garnish with coriander leaves and ginger juliennes. Serve hot.

KADHAI PEAS

SERVES: 4

A chilli hot and colourful dish.

— Ingredients —

Green peas — *900 gms*
Black cardamom powder
— *5 gms/1 tsp*
Black pepper powder
— *8 gms/1²/₃ tsp*
Coriander seeds, crushed
— *15 gms/3 tsp*
Dry fenugreek leaves
(*methi*) — *25 gms/5 tsp*
Garam masala
— *15 gms/3 tsp*
Garlic paste
— *25 gms/5 tsp*
Ginger paste
— *25 gms/5 tsp*
Green coriander, chopped
— *15 gms/3 tsp*
Green chillies, chopped — *5*
Lemon juice — *15 ml/1 tbs*
Oil — *80 ml/¹/₃ cup*
Salt to taste

Red chilli powder
— *10 gms/2 tsp*
Red chillies, whole — *6*
Tomatoes, skinned, chopped
— *350 gms/1³/₄ cups*

— Steps —

1. Heat the oil in a *kadhai/ wok*, add the ginger and garlic pastes and sauté over medium heat for a minute. **2.** Add the whole red chillies, garam masala, red chilli powder, lemon juice

54

and tomatoes and sauté for 5 minutes until the gravy is smooth and well blended.

3. Add the green peas and stir. Season with salt and pepper.

TIPS

Time: Preparation: 10 minutes
Cooking: 15 minutes

To serve: Sprinkle cardamom powder, dry fenugreek leaves, crushed coriander seeds, green chillies and green coriander and serve hot with parantha or roti.

PANEER BIRBALI

SERVES: 4

Cottage cheese curried in tomatoes and garnished with cream.

— Ingredients —

Cottage cheese (*paneer*), block — *1 kg*
Bay leaves (*tej patta*) — *2*
Cashewnuts — *100 gms/¹/₂ cup*
Cinnamon sticks — *3*
Cream — *6 gms/1¹/₃ tsp*
Cumin seeds — *3 gms/²/₃ tsp*
Garlic paste — *40 gms/2²/₃ tbs*
Ginger juliennes — *6 gms/1¹/₃ tsp*
Gram flour or maize flour — *150 gms/³/₄ cup*
Ginger paste — *40 gms/2²/₃ tbs*
Green cardamoms — *3 gms/²/₃ tsp*
Green coriander, chopped — *15 gms/3 tsp*
Mace powder (*javitri*) — *3 gms/²/₃ tsp*
Milk — *50 ml/3¹/₃ tbs*
Oil — *200 ml/1 cup*
Onions, chopped — *100 gms/¹/₂ cup*
Red chilli powder — *10 gms/2 tsp*
Salt to taste
Tomatoes, chopped — *300 gms/1¹/₂ cups*

— Steps —

1. Heat 80 ml (¹/₃ cup) oil in a heavy pan. Add cardamoms, bay leaves, cumin seeds and cinnamon sticks and sauté over medium heat for 30 seconds.
2. Add the ginger and garlic pastes, red chilli powder and onions and sauté for 5 minutes. Add the tomatoes and 1½ cups of water, cover and cook over medium heat for 5-10 minutes. Uncover, stir and cook for another 5 minutes or until oil separates from the gravy.
3. Add mace, salt and three-fourths of the cream. Strain the gravy and keep aside.
4. Mix the gram flour in the milk to make a thick batter. Beat the batter for 3 minutes. Coat the paneer block with the batter. Heat the remaining oil in a pan and shallow fry the block until light brown.
5. Slice the paneer block lengthwise into 4 cm cubes, place on a platter and pour the hot sauce over it.

Time: Preparation: 10 minutes
Cooking: 20 minutes

To serve: Garnish with chopped coriander leaves, ginger juliennes and crushed cashewnuts.

TIPS

SMOKED AUBERGINE

SERVES: 4

Smoked aubergine delicacy, locally known as
Baigan ka Bharta.

— Ingredients —

Aubergines (*baigan*), large, round ones — *1 kg*
Cumin seeds (*jeera*) — *3 gms/²/₃ tsp*
Ginger, chopped — *10 gms/2 tsp*
Green chillies — *2*
Green coriander, chopped — *15 gms/3 tsp*

Oil — *150 gms/³/₄ cup*
Onions, chopped — *120 gms/²/₃ cup*
Paprika powder — *5 gms/1 tsp*
Tomatoes, chopped — *400 gms/2 cups*
Yoghurt — *150 gms/³/₄ cup*
Salt to taste

— Steps —

1. Preheat the oven to 175 ºC (350 ºF). Skewer the aubergines, baste with a little oil and roast in an oven (or charcoal grill or a low flame) until the skin starts peeling off. Immerse the aubergines in water to cool. Remove the skin, the stem and chop the flesh roughly.
2. Heat the oil in a kadhai/wok, add cumin seeds and sauté over medium heat until they begin to crackle.
3. Add onions. Sauté until brown. Add the ginger and stir. Reduce the heat, add yoghurt, paprika, salt and stir.
4. Add the tomatoes and sauté until the oil starts separating from the gravy.
5. Add the chopped aubergines. Sauté for 4-5 minutes. Add green chillies and stir.

TIPS

Time: Preparation: 20 minutes
Cooking: 20 minutes

To serve: Serve hot or cold, garnished with green coriander leaves.

BANANA KOFTA

SERVES: 4

Fried raw banana dumplings in a thick aromatic gravy.

— Ingredients —

Raw bananas — *450 gms*
Cardamoms — *6*
Cinnamon — *1" stick*
Cloves — *4*
Coriander leaves, chopped
— *20 gms/4 tsp*
Cream — *60 ml/¼ cup*
Dough for sealing dish
Garlic paste — *15 gms/1 tbs*
Ginger, chopped fine
— *15 gms/1 tbs*
Ginger paste — *15 gms/1 tbs*
Green chillies — *6*
Oil to deep fry

Honey — *5 ml/1 tsp*
Mace (*javitri*) powder
— *a pinch*
Onions, chopped fine
— *60 gms/¼ cup*
Onions, chopped
— *60 gms/¼ cup*
Red chilli powder
— *5 gms/1 tsp*
Tomatoes, chopped
— *160 gms/²/₃ cup*
White pepper powder
— *2.5 gms/½ tsp*
Salt to
taste

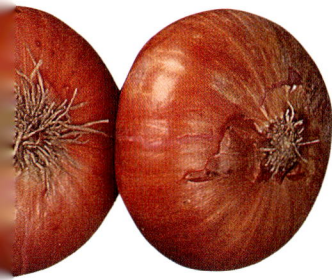

— Steps —

1. Put bananas in a pan, cover with water and boil for 30 minutes. Cool, peel and mash.

2. Mix in the finely chopped onion, ginger, coriander, green chillies, white pepper powder and salt. Divide into 15 portions and roll into balls (*koftas*) between your palms. Deep fry in a kadhai over low heat till golden brown. Keep aside.

3. Remove excess oil from the kadhai, leaving behind 4 tablespoons. Heat oil and crackle cardamoms, cloves and cinnamon in it. Add the roughly chopped onions. Sauté till transparent. Add ginger and garlic pastes and sauté till onions turn brown.

4. Make a purée of the tomatoes in a blender.

5. Add tomato purée, red chilli powder and salt to the kadhai. Stir-cook till oil surfaces.

6. Add 400 ml/1²/₃ cups water. Bring to boil, remove and strain through soup strainer into another pot.

7. Put the pot on fire and bring gravy to boil. Add cream. Remove and add honey.

8. Arrange koftas in an oven proof casserole. Pour gravy over, sprinkle with mace powder, cover and seal dish with dough.

9. Place dish in preheated oven at 275 °F for 8-10 minutes.

TIPS

Time: Preparation: 45 minutes
Cooking: 45 minutes

To serve: Open the seal and serve with boiled rice or paratha.

VEGETABLE KORMA

SERVES: 4

A mixed vegetable delight with the goodness of many fresh vegetables in one dish.

— Ingredients —

Beans, chopped — *100 gms*
Carrots, diced — *100 gms*

Kohlrabi, dried — *100 gms*
Peas, shelled — *100 gms*

Potatoes, diced — *100 gms*
Tomatoes, chopped
— *100 gms*
Bay leaf (*tej patta*) — *2*
Cardamoms — *6*
Cinnamon — *1" stick*
Clarified butter (*ghee*)
— *30 gms/2 tbs*
Cloves — *3*
Coconut, grated
— *160 gms/²/₃ cup*
Coriander leaves, chopped
— *10 gms/2 tsp*

Fennel (*saunf*)
— *10 gms/2 tsp*
Green chillies, chopped — *2*
Ginger, chopped
— *5 gms/1 tsp*
Onions, chopped
— *30 gms/2 tbs*
Poppy seeds (*khus khus*)
— *10 gms/2 tsp*
Salt to taste
Turmeric (*haldi*) powder
— *2.5 gms/¹/₂ tsp*

— *Steps* —

1. Blend coconut, green chillies, onions, ginger, turmeric powder and coriander leaves to a fine paste in a blender.

2. On a hot griddle roast the fennel, cinnamon, cloves, cardamoms and poppy seeds. Cool and put in a blender to make a fine powder.

3. In a pan put just enough water to cover the vegetables along with bay leaves and salt and cook.

4. Once the vegetables are tender and the water evaporated add the coconut-onion paste. Stir-cook for 2-3 minutes.

5. Add the powdered seeds and clarified butter. Stir well for 5 minutes.

TIPS

Time: Preparation: 45 minutes
Cooking: 30 minutes

To serve: Transfer to a dish and serve with any Indian bread.

GLOSSARY

Alu: Potato.

Amchoor: Dried mango powder. Lemon juice may be used as a substitute.

Aniseed (Sweet cumin): Aromatic seeds used in meat dishes.

Aromatic garam masala (Chana masala): Ingredients: Green cardamoms 175 gms; cumin seeds 120 gms; black pepper corns 120 gms; cinnamon (2.5 cms) 25 sticks; cloves 15 gms; nutmegs, 2. Makes 440 gms. Method: Grind all the ingredients to a fine powder. Sieve and store in an airtight container.

Asafoetida (Heeng): A pungent resin used in powdered form.

Baigan (Aubergine, Egg plant, Brinjal): Used whole, or in pieces.

Basmati rice: A fine long-grain rice grown mainly in India.

Bay leaf (Tej patta): An aromatic leaf used for flavouring.

Black beans (Urad dal): A black lentil, used whole or split.

Black lentils (Masoor dal): Also known as red split lentils.

Capsicum: Green bell pepper.

Cardamom, green (Chhoti elaichi): A plant of the ginger family whose seeds are used in flavouring.

Cardamom, large black (Badi elaichi): Used in many vegetable and meat dishes, its black pods are used ground whole.

Carom seeds (Ajwain): Also known as thymol or omum seeds.

Cauliflower (Gobi): Used whole or as flowerets to make a dry curry.

Chaat masala: Ingredients: Cumin seeds 65 gms; black pepper corns, black salt (pounded) and common salt 60 gms each; dry mint leaves 30 gms; carom seeds, asafoetida (pounded) 5 gms each; mango powder 150 gms; ginger powder, yellow chilli powder 20 gms each. Makes 445 gms. Method: Grind cumin seeds, pepper-corns, mint leaves and asafoetida together. Transfer to a bowl, mix remaining ingredients. Sieve and store in an airtight container.

Chillies, green (Hari mirch): Fresh chillies used for flavouring and tempering.

Chillies, whole dried red (Sabut mirch): More pungent than green chillies.

Chilli powder (Mirch pisi): Ground dried red chillies.

Cinnamon (Dalchini): An aromatic bark used as a spice.

Clarified butter (Ghee): Made at home but also available commercially.

Cloves (Lavang): Dried flower bud of a tropical plant, used as a spice.

Coconut, grated fresh: Method: Remove the coconut flesh from the hard shell with a knife and grate.

Coconut milk, fresh: Method: Put 2 cups of grated coconut into a food processor. Add 3 cups of water and blend. Sieve and squeeze out all the liquid. Use liquid. Excellent quality tinned coconut milk is available.

Coconut, creamed: Creamed coconut is easily available and can be converted into coconut milk by adding $^2/_3$ cup hot water to $^1/_3$ cup of creamed coconut.

Coriander, fresh green (Chinese parsley or Hara dhania): A herb used for seasoning and garnishing.

Coriander seeds, whole/ground (Dhania): Seeds of the coriander plant.

Cottage cheese (Paneer): Method: Boil 3 litres of milk. Add the juice of one lemon and stir till the mixture curdles. Remove from the fire. Cover and keep aside for 10 minutes. Strain the mixture through a piece of cheese cloth. Tie the ends of cloth together, squeeze out all the liquid, and place under a heavy weight for a few hours. The cheese (300 gms) is now ready for use.

Cumin seeds (Jeera): Available whole; may be powdered.

Cumin seeds, black (Shah jeera, Kala jeera): A caraway-like seed with a flavour that is more subtle than that of ordinary cumin; to be used sparingly.

Curry leaves, fresh and dried (Kari patta): Highly aromatic leaves. Use fresh.

Dals: Dried lentils. The word is used loosely for all pulses.

Dried milk (Khoya): A milk preparation made by evaporating creamy fresh milk. Use milk powder instead.

Dum cooking: This technique is used to improve the flavour of a dish by the method of sealing the lid, generally with dough and cooking on a low flame.

Fennel seeds (Saunf): These seeds are larger but look and taste like aniseeds.

Fenugreek leaves (Methi): A leafy vegetable, considered to be a great delicacy.

Fenugreek leaves, dried (Kasoori methi): Grown only in the Kasoor region of Pakistan, its dried leaves are used in chicken and lamb preparations.

Fenugreek seeds (Methe): Yellow, square and flat seeds with a bitter flavour.

Garam masala: Ingredients: Cumin seeds 90 gms; black pepper-corns 70 gms; black cardamom seeds 75 gms; fennel seeds 30 gms; green cardamoms 40 gms; coriander seeds 30 gms; cloves, mace powder, black cumin seeds, 20 gms each; cinnamon (2.5 cms) 20 sticks; bay leaves 15 gms; ginger powder 15 gms; nutmegs 3. Makes 445 gms. Method: Grind all the ingredients except the ginger powder. Transfer to a clean bowl, add ginger powder and mix well. Sieve and store in an airtight container.

Ginger (Adrak): A root with a pungent flavour. Peel the skin before use.

Gram flour (Besan): A binding agent, used mainly as a batter.

Mace (Javitri): The outer membrane of nutmeg, used as a flavouring agent.

Maize flour (Makki ka atta): Flour made from Indian corn.

Melon seeds (Magaz): Peeled melon seeds are used in savoury dishes.

Mint leaves (Pudina): A herb, used fresh or dried.

Mustard oil (Sarson ka tel): An edible oil extracted from mustard seeds.

Mustard seeds, black (Sarson): A pungent seed, widely used in Indian food.

Nigella Indica (Kalonji): Used in Indian breads, vegetables and fish.

Nutmeg (Jaiphal): A spice, used grated or ground for flavouring sweets and curies.

Parsley: Can be a substitute for green coriander leaves.

Pistachios (Pista): A dried fruit, used in sweetmeats and biryanis.

Pomegranate seeds (Anardana): Used in savouries, and to give a sour flavour.

Poppy seeds (Khus khus): Tiny white seeds used for flavouring.

Rose water (Gulab jal): A flavouring made of fresh rose petals.

Saffron (Kesar/Zafran): The stigma of the crocus flower, grown in the Kashmir valley. Known as the king of spices, it is used for its rich yellow colouring and flavour. Dissolve in water or warm milk before use.

Sambar powder: Ingredients: Coriander seeds 150 gms; cumin seeds 100 gms; black pepper corns 40 gms; mustard seeds 40 gms; fenugreek seeds 40 gms; red chilli, whole 40 gms; turmeric powder 25 gms; Bengal gram 80 gms; urad dal 80 gms; oil 50 ml; garlic powder 20 gms; ginger powder 20 gms; Makes 600 gms. Method: Heat the oil. Sauté all the ingredients on very low heat until evenly coloured. Cool and grind to a fine powder.

Sesame seeds (Til): An oil-yielding seed used for sweets and savouries.

Split green beans (Moong ki dal): A type of lentil, used split or whole.

Spinach (Palak): A leafy green vegetable.

Tamarind (Imli): A pod-like, sour fruit, used as a souring agent.

Turmeric (Haldi): A root of the ginger family used for colouring, flavouring and for its antiseptic qualities.

Toovar dal (Pigeon peas): Also known as toor or arhar dal.

Vetivier (Kewda): An extract made from the flowers of the kewda (*pandanus*) plant used extensively as a flavouring.

Yoghurt (Dahi): Made from milk and used extensively in curries and biryani. Drained yoghurt can be obtained by drip-drying the yoghurt in a fine muslin or cheesecloth for 4 to 6 hours.